This book is dedicated with love to Callie and Justen who will never know how much they have enriched my life until they have children of their own.
– M. D.

Welcome To My Home The Short Grass Prairie

ISBN 978-0-5789-5516-2

Books may be purchased at special discount prices in bulk or for educational purposes. Please contact your local bookseller or email downing.marlac@gmail.com

Book illustrations and design by Alex Chepelev.
The artist used watercolor and digital techniques to create the illustrations for this book.

First edition, 2021

Welcome to My Home

the Short Grass Prairie

Written by Marla Downing
Illustrated by Alex Chepelev

Welcome to my home.
I'm so glad that you have come.
Would you like to have some fun
on this dew dripped morning

So
WARM
FROM THE
SUN?

Do you think
that you can
bound
like me
across the prairie?

Try it
and you will see
who else lives
here with me.

WAIT! Listen!
Do you HEAR
the BUZZ
of a Bee
in your ear?

LOOK!

The bee is landing on the prarie coneflower there.

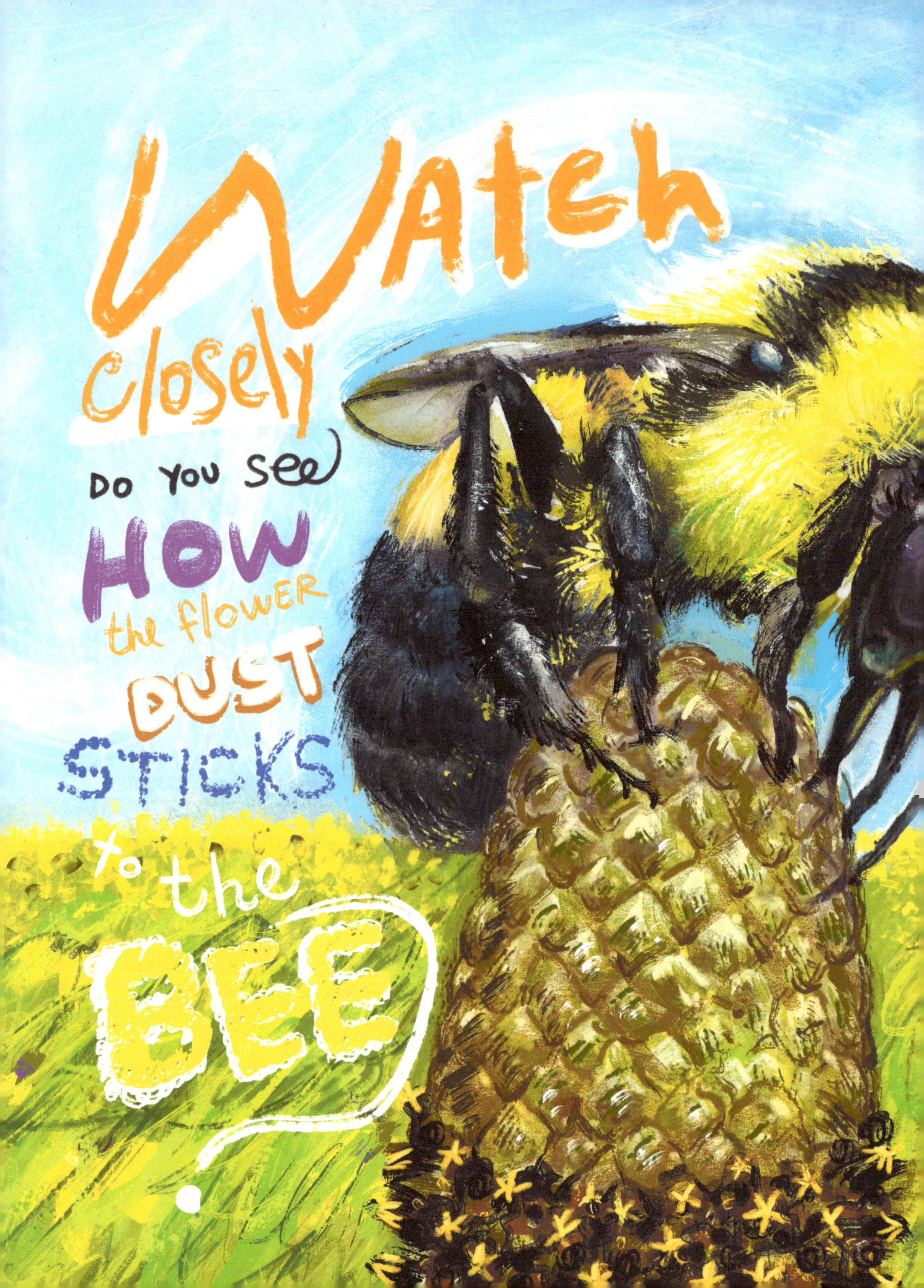
Watch
closely
do you see
HOW
the flower
DUST
STICKS
to the
BEE
?

He will take
that DUST
to ALL the OTHER
Flowers
he
wants
to see

I know
where there is
a TOWN
That is
full of
mounds of
BrOWN,

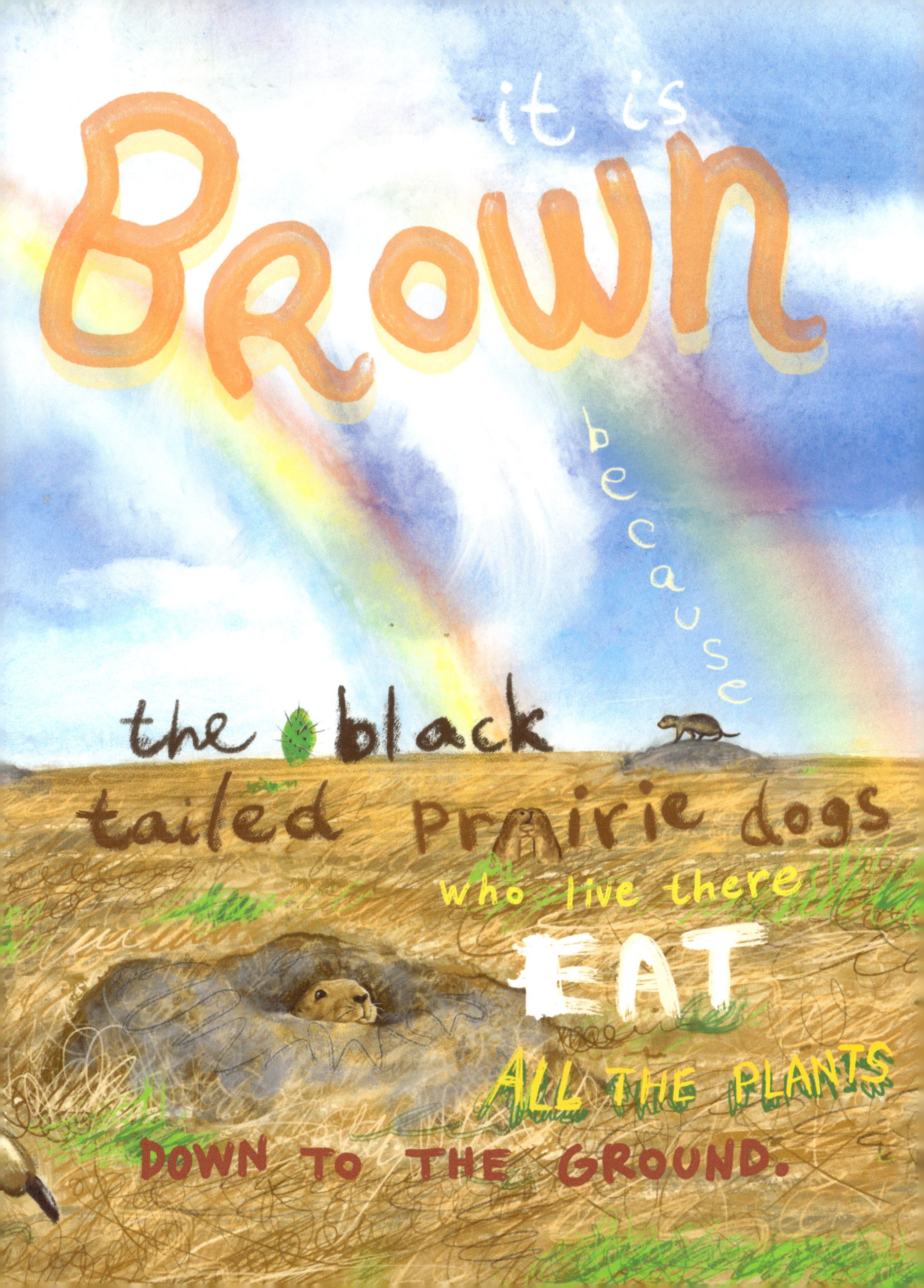
it is
BROWN
because
the black
tailed prairie dogs
who live there
EAT
ALL THE PLANTS
DOWN TO THE GROUND.

The prairie dogs
sure must think
THAT THE PLANTS ARE
YUMMY

Do you suppose
that nibbling
on plants
would feed
your
tummy?

You must be quiet,
Shhh
or soon you will hear

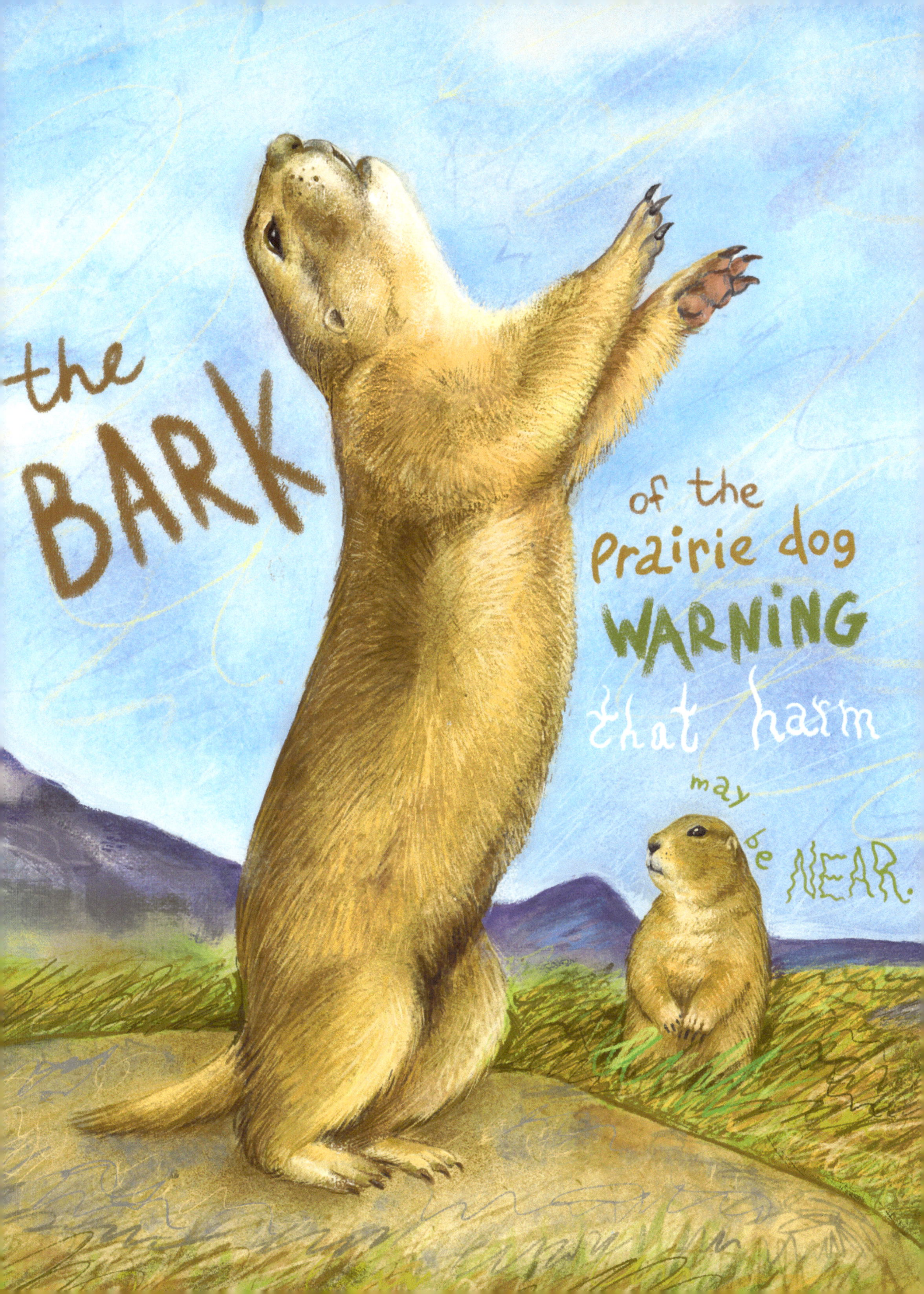
the BARK
of the
prairie dog
WARNING
that harm
may be NEAR.

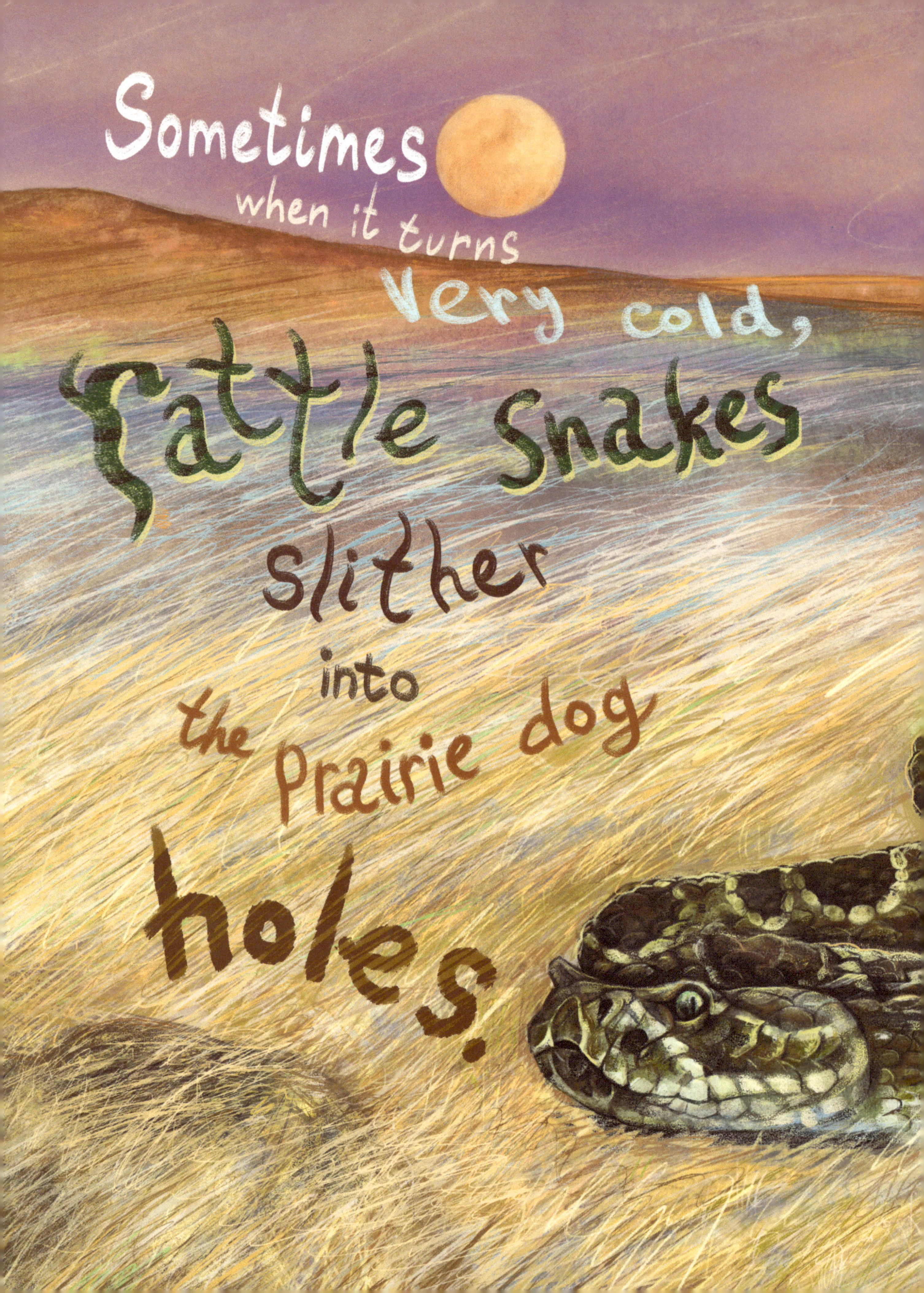
Sometimes
when it turns
very cold,
rattle snakes
slither
into
the prairie dog
holes.

Have you ever tried to move like a Snake?

It makes MY BACK ACHE!

The Snakes snuggle up and get quite cozy

during the long winter of blissful dozing.

The burrowing owl likes to use the holes too.

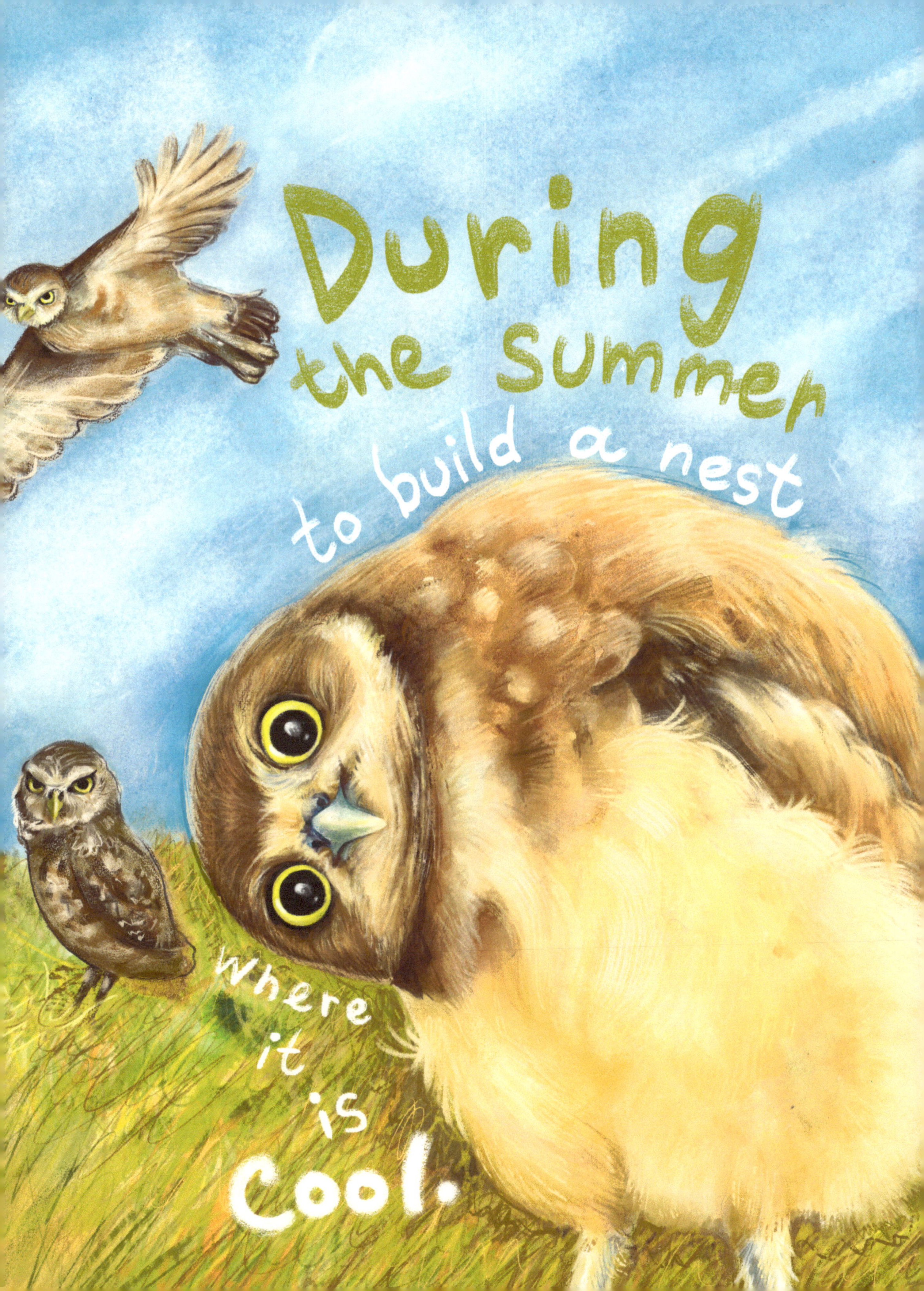
During
the Summer
to build a nest
where
it
is
cool.

It is time
to say
goodbye,
but before you leave
our meadow

try to be AS quick AS
the Swift fox
and see if you
can pounce on your
Shadow!

Enjoy these adorable

prairie animal cards!

www.ingramcontent.com/pod-product-compliance
Ingram Content Group UK Ltd.
Pitfield, Milton Keynes, MK11 3LW, UK
UKHW061940050826
14089UKWH00045BA/210